Alabama

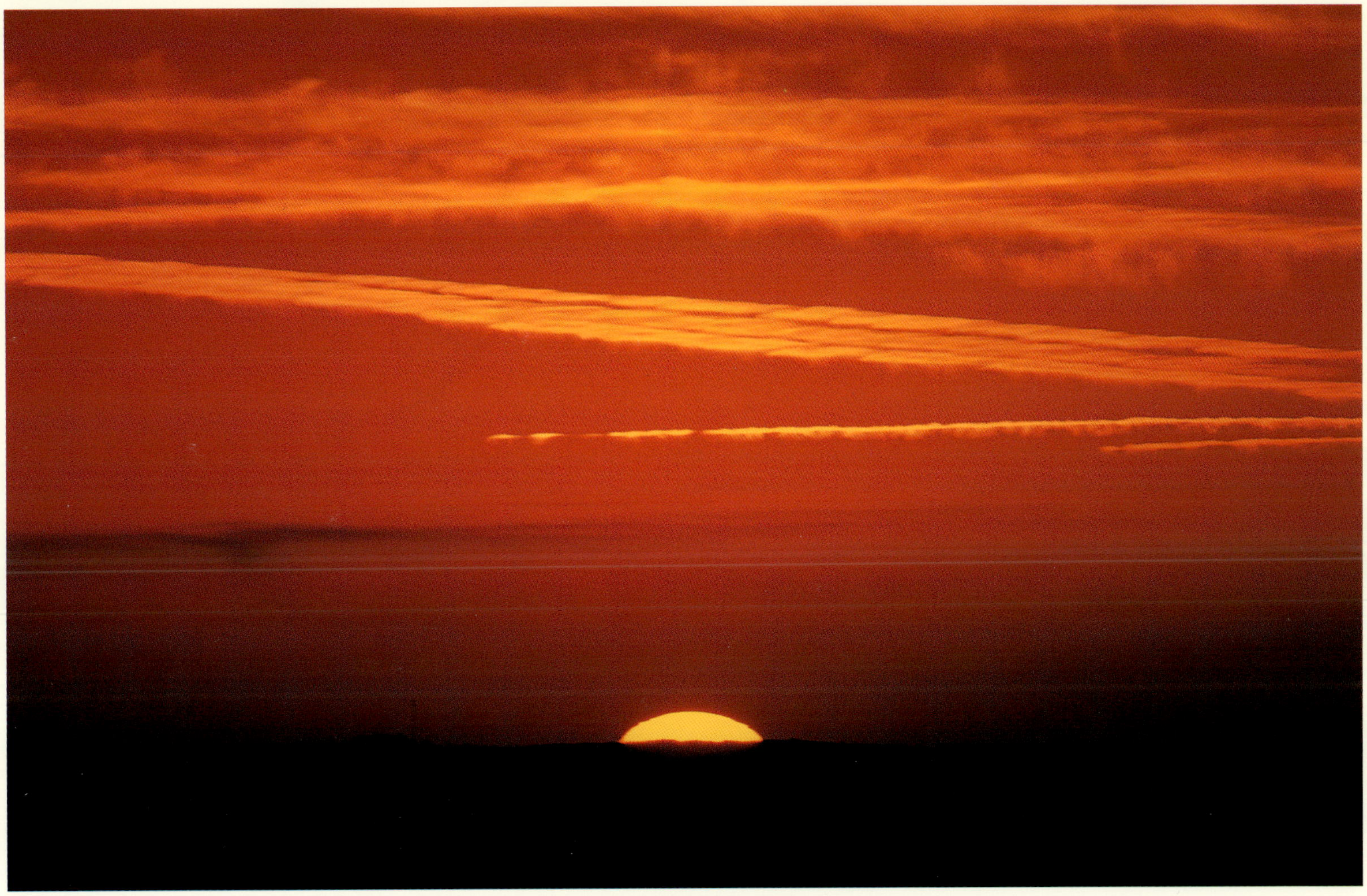

Photography by Charles Seifried

FARCOUNTRY PRESS

ISBN: 1-56037-277-X

© 2004 Farcountry Press

Photographs © Charles Seifried

Photos of Baldwin County courtesy of The First National Bank of Baldwin County.

This book may not be reproduced in whole or in part by any means (with the exception of short quotes for the purpose of review) without the permission of the publisher.

For more information on our books write: Farcountry Press, P.O. Box 5630, Helena, MT 59604; call (800) 821-3874; or visit www.farcountrypress.com

Created, produced, and designed in the United States.

Printed in China.

ABOVE: High Falls, DeKalb County.

TITLE PAGE: A dramatic sunset near Birmingham.

FRONT COVER: Little River Falls.

FRONT FLAP: Soft sands and a soft chair await at gulf shores.

BACK COVER: Horse farm near Foley.

Introduction *by Charles Seifried*

Alabama has been my home now for over twenty-six years. Throughout my life I have traveled all over the world and visited nearly all the states of this great nation. I landed here in Decatur, Alabama—I have lived here longer than any other place.

When I first moved here, I longed for the exotic scenery of my childhood. Memories of the high mountains in northern Luzon and flame-tree blossoms in the Philippines still held me. Not knowing what Alabama had to offer, I decided to seek solace in the Great Smoky Mountains. Upon the urging of a friend, I began exploring Bankhead National Forest, and over the course of my years here I found many hidden natural treasures just waiting to be photographed. This state of sweet rolling hills, red dirt, and lush country fields has a lot to offer. The soothing breezes, misty mountains, and the rivers and their winding tributaries are only a few of the many joys I have experienced in this wonderful state.

Sipsey Wilderness, in Bankhead National Forest, has become one of my favorite places to visit in northern Alabama. There I have found deep canyons filled with five different types of flowering large-leaf magnolias, huge holly trees, large yellow and white poplars, and an abundance of hemlocks. Waterfalls by the hundreds cascade down through limestone canyons that sprawl throughout the region. The largest tree in the state, a huge poplar, is located deep in one of these prehistoric-looking canyons. It's a pleasant day hike to reach this state treasure.

Throughout Alabama's forests are signs left behind by the region's Native American tribes. Petroglyphs on tree bark and limestone rocks abound throughout the state. The Creek, Chickasaw, Choctaw, and Cherokee inhabited this area for centuries. While walking through the deep canyons and witnessing their marks upon the land, you can almost feel their ancient presence. Moundville, Alabama, has huge Native American burial mounds that precede known tribes.

In the north, the scenic Tennessee River weaves it way across the state. One of the largest rivers in the United States, it offers excellent fishing and boating in addition to serving as a refuge for all types of ducks, geese, egrets, blue herons, deer, and other wildlife. As soon as the March winds blow, we are out on the river in our kayaks and canoes. Sweetly scented water lilies line the waters edge, and occasionally you might see an alligator silently gliding along. The river gives us plenty of backwaters, including the Wheeler Wildlife Refuge, which hosts thousands of waterfowl traveling the north–south flyway every year. Ducks and geese just pour in and it is quite a sight. The state's many rivers and lakes make it a prime destination for those seeking to fish small- and large-mouth bass.

Alabama is also known for its stunning coastline—Gulf Shores has some of the whitest sands I have ever seen. The water is wonderful, and after a day at the beach swimming or looking for sea shells you can eat at one of the many fine restaurants and stay in one of the condominiums that line the beachfront.

There are golf courses all the way from Mobile to Huntsville. Alabama is proud to have the Robert Trent Jones Golf Trail, which has some of the finest golf courses in the world. While photographing these courses I have run into people from all over the North who love to come down and play in a warmer climate with beautiful settings.

Alabama's cities offer an energetic contrast to the peaceful natural environs. Birmingham is a city alive with a healthy spirit. Music, theater, and arts flourish around its thriving downtown, which is supported by ethnic restaurants and wonderful specialty stores. The capital city of Montgomery houses the nationally acclaimed Alabama Shakespeare Festival, where performances draw people from all over the world. Huntsville is one of the most progressive cities in the Southeast. It is supported by major high-tech firms that are involved in defense and space contracting. The clean industries in Huntsville have given it a reputation for being a desirable place to live.

As I travel throughout Alabama, I realize what a great place in which I live and how much this state has to offer. Whether I am playing golf, climbing the rocks of Mt. Cheaha, hiking the trails of the Sipsey Wilderness, or sailing on the Gulf, I am glad to be in Alabama.

A gentle stream near Decatur.

LEFT: White-tailed buck cautiously surveys his surroundings in Bankhead National Forest.

BELOW: The crisp, cool air brings out the warm hues of fall in a northern Alabama forest.

A busy railyard in Tuscumbia.

The stunning view from Point Clear.

LEFT: A barefooted stroll through a garden.

BELOW: Vibrant spring flowers line the path leading to a stunning pavilion at the Huntsville Botanical Gardens.

FACING PAGE: This hot-air balloon glides above the furrowed farmland near Mooresville.

Eagle Creek Falls cuts through the forest depths of Bankhead National Forest.

Looking out from behind the glittering curtain of Sougahoagbee Falls.

Aerial view of the U.S. Space and Rocket Center, Huntsville.

LEFT: A flicker, or yellowhammer, the state bird of Alabama. Since the Civil War, Alabama has also been known as the "Yellowhammer State."

BELOW: A bright winter day along Cranal Road just outside the Sipsey Wilderness Area; the nearly 26,000 acres of protected forest is closed to motor vehicles but open to a host of recreational activities.

Civil War buffs reenact a dramatic battle near Decatur.

The densely forested uplands of the Little River Canyon, one of the most spectacular spots in the southern Appalachians.

Sunset on Smith Lake, one of the South's most pristine lakes.

ABOVE: The 1844 Bridgetender's Bed and
Breakfast overlooks the Alabama River.

RIGHT: Deceptively delicate pitcher plants—
a sweet but deadly trap for unsuspecting
insects.

FACING PAGE: Sand Rock, popular with
climbers, and Weiss Lake on the horizon.

A quiet hay field near Decatur.

Kayaking through the backwaters of the Tennessee River near Stevenson.

The sun sets on this pastoral scene near Neel.

RIGHT: These acrobats of aviation fly in formation at the Courtland Air Show.

BELOW: A pleasant mix of deciduous and coniferous trees near Smith Lake.

A shrimp boat anchors at a promising location in Alabama waters.

An isolated oasis of serenity, Little River Falls.

ABOVE: A kayaker negotiates the rapids on Locust Fork River, cherished for its cultural heritage, scenic beauty, and recreational opportunities.

RIGHT: Day's end near Scottsboro silhouettes rolling hills against a citrus sky.

FACING PAGE: Just one of the beautiful greens
at Cambian Ridge Golf Course in Greenville.

BELOW: A pecan grove in Baldwin County. Mobile
and Baldwin Counties are the leading producers
of the state nut of Alabama.

Constructed in 1975, the Von Braun Center in Huntsville is a handsome presence on the waterfront.

LEFT: The simple yet stunning blossoms
of the morning glory, Decatur.

BELOW: A lone blue heron roams the backwaters of the Wheeler Wildlife Refuge.

RIGHT: A wren makes a chilly perch on these icy limbs.

BELOW: The Locust Fork, a canoeist's paradise.

FACING PAGE: The hallowed passageways of Fort Morgan, constructed from 1819 to 1834, which stood in defense of Mobile Bay during the Civil War.

ABOVE: This mail carrier has few dogs to contend with on his route along the Magnolia River.

LEFT: Field near Andalusia.

The ivory beaches and emerald waves of Gulf Shores, on the Gulf of Mexico.

ABOVE: With a crack of the sail, this boat glides gracefully through the Mobile Bay waters off Point Clear.

LEFT: These two bridges reach across the Tennessee River toward Huntsville.

ABOVE: Returning from an afternoon ride, Danville.

FACING PAGE: Water tupelo trees emerge from water lily-blanketed
Blackwell Swamp, an excellent area for bird watching.

Autumn arrives at this farm near Danville.

LEFT: This proud cardinal's bright plumage gives away its position in the bare bushes.

BELOW: Tools of the trade—fly fishing on Borden Creek.

With a population of more than a million, modern Birmingham is the state's largest city.

ABOVE: Walking through the tall, cool grass on a blissful summer day.

FACING PAGE: Little River slices its way through pristine forest.

ABOVE: At 4 feet in height, and with a wingspan of 7 feet, the great blue heron is the largest heron in the United States.

FACING PAGE: The gentle cascades of Eagle Creek Falls, Sipsey Wilderness.

ABOVE: The vibrant petals of this fuschia seem to burst from the stem, Bellingrath Gardens. Originally created as a private fishing camp by Walter Bellingrath, the gardens are now open to the public.

FACING PAGE: Anglers get an early start fishing for small- and large-mouth bass on the Tennessee River.

ABOVE: The stately countenance of the Tuscumbia Courthouse.

RIGHT: Orange Beach, Gulf Shores.

A classic sunset on the calm waters south of Point Clear.

ABOVE: A healthy crop of soybeans near Baldwin City.

FACING PAGE: The uniquely medieval Shrine of the Most Blessed Sacrament,
a Catholic church in Hanceville.

Streams of water fall like moonbeams at Caney Creek Falls in Bankhead National Forest.

RIGHT: Capitol Hill Golf Course in Prattville, one of twenty-one beautiful courses that make up the Robert Trent Jones Golf Trail.

BELOW: An inviting bed of violas at the Huntsville Botanical Gardens.

ABOVE: Jesse Owens, who competed in the 1936 Olympics in Germany, was the first American in the history of Olympic track and field to win four gold medals in a single Olympics. This tribute to the athlete is at the Museum of Jesse Owens in Danville.

LEFT: This placid pond near DeSoto Falls reflects the dense woods that enshroud it.

LEFT: You can lean on me; friends for life.

BELOW: The manicured grounds of Windy Hill.

FACING PAGE: With its low canopy of trees, Red Bank Road near Decatur is almost enclosed in a tunnel of greenery.

ABOVE: This lone golden leaf guilds the wet, black rocks at the bottom of a torrential falls in Bankhead National Park.

FACING PAGE: Visitors flock to Gulf Shores to take in the incomparable weather and pristine beaches.

A crisp winter sunset on the Wheeler Wildlife Refuge.

LEFT: The bright buds of crimson clover and buttercups.

BELOW: Beavers create a mound of mud and wood, burrow into the mound from underwater, and then hollow out the mound, creating a den. This beaver has taken up residence in Blackwell Swamp.

FACING PAGE: The North Fork of Caney Creek has eroded through layers of sandstone and limestone.

LEFT: A bounty of spring flora found in Bankhead National Forest.

BELOW: Helen Keller was born here in Tuscumbia on June 27, 1880. Visitors from across America flock here to tour the home.

FACING PAGE: The Judge, a course on the Robert Trent Jones Golf Trail, sits on the bank of the scenic Alabama River.

The wide open highway near Gulf Shores.

LEFT: The USS *Alabama*, or the "Mighty A," is displayed proudly in Mobile. The ship was a part of several key battles during World War II and, after surrender documents were signed, led the American fleet into Tokyo Bay in 1945.

BELOW: The moon rises in the quiet of early evening near Florence.

The sun slips toward the horizon, as seen from Mt. Cheaha
in Talladega National Forest.

RIGHT: Botanical wonders await at Bellingrath Gardens.

BELOW: An Argentinian polo player races down the field at the Blue Water Polo Club.

FACING PAGE: The Smitherman House in Selma is listed on the National Register of Historic Places.

This wheat field near Massey is ready for harvest.

ABOVE: The broad expanse of the Tennesee River.

FACING PAGE: Bare branches seem to reach for the wintery sky that silhouettes them.

Guntersville Lake, located on the Tennessee River, is a 30-mile-long
body of water created by Guntersville Dam.

RIGHT: Lazy summer days spent in Birmingham's Oak Mountain State Park make for treasured childhood memories.

BELOW: This field near Decatur is ready for planting.

FOLLOWING PAGES: The Little River wends its way through rock outcroppings.

Sailboats line the shore at Point Clear.

ABOVE: Barges move up the Tennessee River near Browns Ferry.

FACING PAGE: The last moments of daylight reflected in the water near Scottsboro.

FACING PAGE: This black Labrador retriever has his eye on the prize.

BELOW: Peering through spindly branches at a Thompson Creek swimming hole.

ABOVE: Headed ashore after a day of boating in the beautiful Gulf of Mexico.

FACING PAGE: Sand Island Lighthouse, built in 1873, is Alabama's only coastal lighthouse.

RIGHT: The General Joe Wheeler Home contains memorabilia of this famous general of the Confederate Army and member of the U.S. House of Representatives.

BELOW: Cyclists at Oak Mountain State Park, one of the best bicycling areas in the state.

FACING PAGE: Searching for treasures on a Gulf Shores beach.

With thousands of farms, like this one near Madison, cotton is a multi-billion-dollar industry in Alabama.

Sun glints on Sougahoagbee Falls.

Verdant soybean field near Mooresville.

ABOVE: Canoeing through bald cypress trees in Coffee Slough, near Florence.

RIGHT: The elegant white trillium is also known as wake-robin, as it seems to announce the arrival of robins in early spring.

One of many delightfully inviting paths in Bellingrath Gardens, south of Mobile.

ABOVE: From the cover of a fallen limb, this frog surveys the shore of the Tennessee River.

FACING PAGE: Hiking through a North Caney Creek box canyon.

The warm sands of Gulf Shores.

RIGHT: A paint mare and her foal enjoy the last fleeting moments of daylight.

BELOW: An old building succumbs to time and ever-encroaching trees near Madison.

View of the Gulf of Mexico from Gulf Shores.

The tiered cascades of DeSoto Falls.

ABOVE: Camping on the bank of Eagle Creek.

LEFT: Daybreak near Anniston.

Oak trees filter out sunlight along this farm road in Baldwin County.

Cruising the waters of the Tennessee River, tinged golden by the sun.